Introduction.

Many presences, on our well-shaped planet, are worthy of celebration. Sydney Harbour Bridge, perhaps; the seascapes of Turner and music of Delius; the fleeting beauty of a rainbow; the relentless reason of scientists; but few more so than the marvel we call the eyebrow. In a world requiring asymmetry, our higher feature offers communication which might have caused the great linguist, Michel Thomas, to hurl his trusted tape-recorder, from the Pont d'Avignon. Elevated in great works of art and surely essential to the golden age of Hollywood, such paintbrushes of thought and emotion should be cherished and preserved, with all the vigour we afford to democracy, human rights and the article for play commonly referred to as bubble-wrap.

My inspiration, for this work, was electronically born. The day had been gloomy, with the apparent staleness that typifies early January;

then she was there; smiling from the home-page of my laptop, with a brow slightly raised. *Eyebrow Magic Video: the girl with an unusual talent,* read the caption; and intrigued, by the cheeky 'get a load of this' look, in her eyes, I accepted an invitation to click. The video was a joy; her ability remarkable; and it brightened my day to see those two splendid features dance, in perfect union with an exotic and lilting soundtrack. It was an achievement, too, I could well appreciate; for I hazily recall, at around the age of five, or six, attempting to conjure my own brand of eyebrow magic, before a mirror. The undertaking was ambitious and yet, without wishing to seem immodest, I did meet with some success; to the extent that I could perplex a few classmates, with my new found ability. An underachiever I may, perhaps, have been, but let it be remembered that, in the eyebrow stakes, I was the front-runner. Getting them to alternate was the breakthrough. I mean, most people can raise just the one and anyway, Sir Roger Moore had recently taken over, as Bond, so uncles, aunts, next-door-neighbours and probably even a few Persian cats, were all giving it a whirl (then again, maybe not, but more of that later). The real trick, though, was to get them flowing, smoothly; without assuming an ungainly expression, or dragging each side of the mouth along, for the ride. Those final criteria were my downfall. I simply couldn't master the detail; which is why I feel compelled to salute the aforementioned *YouTube* star, by way of these pages.

Chapter 1   **Harnessing the Brow**

To proponents of creationism, the existence of eyebrows may seem a gift, because they appear to have been placed there, for no reason greater than decoration; yet those with a healthy interest in evolution can provide answers. Certainly, it seems that man's facial coverage receded, leaving remnants upon the lower forehead and a popular view is that they were left there to provide protection from rain. Hardly something to please the likes of Hollywood legend, Gene Kelly, but welcomed by many others and useful in averting the clouding of vision that might have led early humans to hunt, let's say, a buffalo-shaped rock, rather than the animal itself. Furthermore, they might help to deal with sweat. But, there must be more, because eyebrows are muscled, so we can move them, even alternately; and their boldness tends to remain, even when our other hairs have whitened, or been lost. Do they exist, then, as the great broadcaster Sir David Attenborough has suggested, to send messages, of acknowledgement? "If", he has said, "we raise them, quickly, while looking at someone who is too far away to conveniently address with speech, it's a sign that we've registered the other person's presence and are content that they should be around."

Clearly, then, the case for evolved eyebrows is both logical and clear.

But what of the articles themselves? How are they constructed and what distinguishes them from our other remaining hair? Well, the growth cycle, for a start. Not only are eyebrows comprised of the slowest-growing hair found on our bodies, but each strand remains in place for little more than four months, before being replaced. The number of hairs, within each, can vary, but the average is about two hundred and fifty, while the number of follicles exceeds five hundred. Furthermore, close inspection reveals a more acute angle of growth than elsewhere, rendering the hairs much flatter against the skin; together with directional variations, to form an almost woven effect. Again, then, evolution has played something of a blinder; or not, as the case may be. The greater abundance of brow hair among men is easily explained; their having been life's hunters. But cultural developments are more complex.

Copious plucking among western females should not surprise us, because it accentuates a difference between the sexes, but why, then, did eighteenth century women seek to swell the growth of their eyebrows, with bushy attachments, and why is the frequently maligned mono-brow, or uni-brow, if you prefer, considered attractive, in parts of Asia, when worn by females? Moreover, in Iran, many women join their eyebrows, with kohl liner, or kajal pens. One explanation is that, with virginity highly prized there, available females seek to distinguish themselves from more mature, plucking, individuals. But it's by no means clear. More perplexingly, ancient-Egyptian priests sought to rid their bodies of hair, including those of their eyebrows, but rather than seek to fathom the ways of mysticism, I'll move swiftly on. The mono-brow thing has, though, a chequered reputation, thanks, in part, to Victorian criminologist, Cesare Lombroso, who voiced his opinion that it should be seen as an indicator of criminality. But, were he still alive, television viewers may draw his attention to *Sesame Street*'s Bert, who has, I understand, a soundly respectable history, as does the similarly mono-browed Norman the Diesel Engine, from Wilbert Awdry's *Thomas (the tank engine) and Friends*; and so I rest my case.

Were it only that simple; for it seems that, wherever there's a villain, in literature, there's something akin to a hairy caterpillar on his forehead. Charles Dickens knew the game and played it, when creating his Fagin:

"The boy's right," remarked Fagin, looking covertly round, and knitting his shaggy eyebrows, into a hard knot. "You're right, Oliver, you're right; they will think you have stolen 'em. Ha! ha!" chuckled the Jew, rubbing his hands; "it couldn't have happened better, if we had chosen our time!"

With Heathcliff, in *Wuthering Heights,* the association is less clear, because his character is more complex; yet a brooding aspect is beyond question; and the character of Nelly, when attempting to remind him of his place in the world, quickly calls attention to his upper furnishings:

"Oh, Heathcliff, you are showing a poor spirit! Come to the glass, and I'll let you see what you should wish. Do you mark those two lines, between your eyes; and those thick brows, that, instead of rising arched, sink in the middle; and that couple of black fiends, so deeply buried, who never open their windows boldly, but lurk glinting under them, like devil's spies? Wish and learn to smooth away the surly wrinkles, to raise your lids frankly, and change the fiends to confident, innocent angels, suspecting and doubting nothing, and always seeing friends, where they are not sure of foes. Don't get the expression of a vicious cur, that appears to know the kicks it gets are its desert, and yet hates all the world; as well as the kicker, for what it suffers."

In Henry Fielding's most popular work, Tom Jones's ultimate love, Sophia Western, sports eyebrows that are *'full, even, and arched beyond the power of art to imitate'* while, in *The Miller's Tale*, Chaucer tell us that his alluring Alisoun's eyebrows, are, in contrast with her morning milk-coloured apron, *'black as any sloe'* (for urbanites, the comparison relates to the fruit of the blackthorn shrub). Considering the bawdiness that ensues, it is, perhaps, an aptly fruity comparison.

And Niccolo Modrussa understood, it seems, the brow's ability to introduce the negative and applied it well, when describing Vlad the Impaler:

 'He was not very tall, but very stocky and strong, with a cold and terrible appearance, a strong and aquiline nose, swollen nostrils, a thin reddish face, in which very long eyelashes framed large wide-open green eyes; the bushy black eyebrows made them appear threatening.

We should note, too, Bram Stoker's Dracula:

'His face was strong; a very strong; aquiline, with high bridge of the thin nose and peculiarly arched nostrils; with lofty domed forehead, and hair growing scantily round the temple, but profusely elsewhere. His eyebrows were very massive, almost meeting over the nose, and with bushy hair, that seemed to curl in its own profusion.

All very descriptive, but, surely, no match for Claudia's take, on her father, in Toni Morrison's *The Bluest Eye*. She saw his face as a study, into which winter moved and presided. His eyes became, to her, a cliff of snow, threatening to avalanche; with eyebrows bent, like black limbs of leafless trees.

We may choose other measures of quantity; but Charles Dickens, in his 1843 classic, *A Christmas Carol*, was clearly keen that readers should fully appreciate the feast's fulsomeness:

"...indeed, as Mrs. Cratchit said, with great delight (surveying one small atom of a bone, upon the dish) they hadn't ate it all at last! Yet every one had had enough, and the youngest Cratchits, in particular, were steeped in sage and onion, to the eyebrows."

Further to Dickens' interest, the brow; being, of course, central to the universe; may, eventually, become the point from which all distances are measured; all the way to the faintest of galaxies that circle around it and beyond.

Back on terra firma, HG Wells; in *War of The Worlds*, assured us of implicit humanity in the wife of his unnamed journalist; as he described, to her, a Martian invader, loitering in Surrey's commuter-belt, with no need of even an off-peak return:

"There is one thing," I said, to allay the fears I had aroused; "they are the most sluggish things I ever saw crawl. They may keep the pit and kill people, who come near them, but they cannot get out of it. . . . but the horror of them!"' "Don't, dear!" said my wife, knitting her brows and putting her hand on mine.'

And Wells was sure, also, to dehumanise the creature she'd learned of:

'Those who have never seen a living Martian can scarcely imagine the strange horror of its appearance. The peculiar V-shaped mouth, with its pointed upper lip, the absence of brow-ridges, the absence of a chin beneath the wedge-like lower lip.'

Like the Martians imagined by Wells, cats do not possess eyebrows; at least, in the conventional sense. The long hairs above their eyes, are better described as additional whiskers. They are there neither for signalling, nor to protect the animal's vision from liquids, but act, instead, as sensors, enabling it to pass, safely, through narrow openings.

We might, however, be thankful, to T S Eliot, who, in *Old Possum's Book of Practical Cats* (upon which Andrew Lloyd Webber based his smash-hit musical, *Cats*), reminded us, that the word 'brow' also refers to the lower forehead, in general. His Mcavity; a tall and thin ginger cat, with a tendency to disappear, had, we are informed, eyes sunken in and a brow deeply lined, with thought.

Wilfred Owen utilized the forehead, too; though for much more than a thoughtful cat. In his *Anthem for Doomed Youth,* he expressed the heartbreak of human loss:

What candles may be held to speed them all?
Not in the hands of boys but in their eyes
Shall shine the holy glimmers of goodbyes.
The pallor of girls' brows shall be their pall;
Their flowers of tenderness of patient minds,
And each slow dusk a drawing-down of blinds.

In contrast, Robbie Burns, upon writing *Tam O'Shanter*, gave his brooding farmers' wife tempestuous features:

We think na on the lang Scots miles,

The mosses, waters, slaps, and styles,

That lie between us and our hame,

Where sits our sulky sullen dame.

Gathering her brows like gathering storm,

Nursing her wrath to keep it warm.

Meanwhile, the 'wreathless' brow of Samuel Taylor Coleridge is shown to us, in *Work Without Hope*, for reasons more akin to those of the war poets. To speak of fruitless toil and the bleak path he must continue to tread:

With lips unbrightened, wreathless brow, I stroll:

And would you learn the spells that drowse my soul?

Work without Hope draws nectar in a sieve,

And Hope without an object cannot live.

Poirot's eyebrows danced their way through the novels of Agatha Christie. When he was on the scene, they were up and down, like the proverbial yoyo:

'Hercule Poirot's eyebrows rose' it's said, in *Hercule Poirot's Christmas*, when someone had half-inched an ornamental cannon ball. They rose again, though more slightly, within *The Adventure of the Christmas Pudding*, as he noted an eccentric side to the millionaire, behind the door; and in *Dead Man's Folly* they *'shot up',* as the memory of Mrs Ariadne Oliver's windswept grey hair and eagle profile rose, in his mind. Well, you can't keep a great man down; or not, at least, his eyebrows.

And should you doubt the brow's allure, note, perhaps, that Thomas Hardy cottoned onto it, more than a century ago. *Tess, of the d'Urbevilles*, when seeking to uglify herself *'by a felicitous thought, took a handkerchief from her bundle and tied it round her face, under her bonnet, covering her chin and half her cheeks and temples, as if she were suffering from toothache. Then with her little scissors, by the aid of a pocket looking-glass, she mercilessly nipped her eyebrows off, and thus insured against aggressive admiration she went on her uneven way'.*

Thus, she threw her heart, again, toward an absent husband and shunned other men.

We might ponder D H Lawrence's opinion, of brows, found in the south-west, because they seemed, to him, quite distinct; as we can tell, from this description, in his *England, My England* work:

'The woman, after a moment's hesitation, took her seat again at the table with the card-players. She had noticed the man: a big fine fellow, well dressed; a stranger. But he spoke with that Cornish-Yankee accent she accepted as the natural twang among the miners. The stranger put his foot on the fender and looked into the fire. He was handsome, well coloured, with well-drawn Cornish eyebrows, and the usual dark, bright, mindless Cornish eyes. He seemed abstracted in thought.'

As for Shakespeare… well, he seems to have shared my own preoccupation. References to those wonders of the lower forehead are scattered all over the place. There are wrinkled brows (*King John*), brows of much distraction (*The Winter's Tale*), unsmirched brows (*Hamlet*), brows of woe (also *Hamlet*), brows with moles upon them (*Twelfth Night*), brows full of discontent (*Richard II*), square brows (*Pericles, Prince of Tyre*), smoothed brows (*Henry VI*), sad brows (*Julius Caesar*), black brows of the night (*King John*), blacker brows (*The Winter's Tale*), brows knitted by the great duke Humphrey (*Henry VI*), solemn brows (King John), brows containing a discerning eye (*King Lear*), brows that cannot be mended by praise (*Love's Labours Lost*), warlike brows (*Richard III*), brows upon which shame is ashamed to sit (*Romeo and Juliet*), outfaced brows (*King John*), bloody brows (*Coriolanus*), brows of grace (*Macbeth*), gold-bound brows (also *Macbeth*), brows of justice (*Henry IV*), fair ladies' brows, kissed by happy masks (*Romeo and Juliet*), brows with right arched beauty (*The Merry Wives of Windsor*), brows circled by imperial metal (*Richard III*), brows with angry spots glowing on them (*Julius Caesar*), brows with moody frontiers (*Henry IV*), brows with beads of sweat standing upon them (*Henry IV*), dangerous brows (*Julius Caesar*), brows of Egypt (*A Midsummer Night's Dream*), brows with grace seated upon them

17

(*Hamlet*), bent brows (*Henry VI*), stained brows (*Henry IV*), brows prepared to frown (*Coriolanus*), brows bound with victorious wreaths (*Richard III*), bare brows (*As You Like It*), brows that o'erwhelm (*Henry V*), confident brows (*Henry IV*), brows within a golden crown (*Cymbeline*), rubbed brows (*Hamlet*), held brows (*Loves Labour's Lost*), broken brows (*Juliet*), unkind brows (*The Taming of the Shrew*), brows of heaven (*Love's Labour's Lost*), stern brows (*As You Like It*), brows with garlands on them (*Julius Caesar*), brows of youth (*Henry VI*), mourning brows of progeny (*Love's Labour's Lost*), vaulty brows (*King John*), gentle brows (*King John*), contracted and pursed brows (*Othello*), baby brows (*Macbeth*), harlot brows (*The Comedy of Errors*), hardened brows (The Winter's Tale), towns with resisting brows (*King John*), velvet brows (*Love's Labour's Lost*), brows that become nothing (*The Merry Wives of Windsor*), inky brows (*As You Like It*) and imitated brows (*Love's Labour's Lost*); not neglecting to mention the giant clump of hair suspended above the door of Ann Hathaway's cottage; well, alright then, but I think it's fair to say his interest in them was exceptional.

Some mentions are, though, difficult to understand; and Juliet's wait for her 'black-browed night' perplexes me. Clearly, night is more than welcome, but are we to see it as a friendly visitor, in human form, or a darkening of the landscape, as daylight fades upon the brow of a hill? Those with more years of study may have the answer, but my own inkling is that the Bard meant both:

'Come, night; come, Romeo; come, thou day in night;
For thou wilt lie upon the wings of night
Whiter than new snow upon a raven's back
Come, gentle night; come, loving, black-brow'd night;
Give me my Romeo; and, when he shall die,
Take him and cut him out in little stars,
And he will make the face of heaven so fine
That all the world will be in love with night
And pay no worship to the garish sun.'

While the brow may, perhaps, have a language of its own, there are clear limitations, as we can learn from Madame Campan's Memoirs of Marie Antoinette:

19

"One day, I, unintentionally, threw this poor lady into a terrible agony. The Queen was receiving I know not whom; - some persons just presented, I believe; the lady of honour, the Queen's tirewoman, and the ladies of the bedchamber, were behind the Queen. I was near the throne, with the two women on duty. All was right; at least I thought so. Suddenly I perceived the eyes of Madame de Noailles, fixed on mine. She made a sign, with her head, and then raised her eyebrows, to the top of her forehead, lowered them, raised them again, then began to make little signs, with her hand. From all this pantomime, I could easily perceive that something was not as it should be; and as I looked about on all sides, to find out what it was, the agitation of the Countess kept increasing. The Queen, who perceived all this, looked at me with a smile; I found means to approach her Majesty, who said to me in a whisper, 'Let down your lappets, or the Countess will expire.' All this bustle arose from two unlucky pins which fastened up my lappets, whilst the etiquette of costume said 'Lappets hanging down.'"

Upon meeting him, sculptor and cousin to Sir Winston Churchill, Clare Sheridan, was impressed, by the Russian revolutionary Leon

Trotsky's lupine features. The encounter she described, quite vividly, in her diary. Trotsky's eyes, according to Sheridan, were much talked of, in Russia, where he was referred to as the wolf. *"His nose was straight; and when seen full-face, he could have been Mephisto. His eyebrows rose, at an angle and his lower region tapered, she recalled, to a pointed and defiant beard."*

We're left to wonder how things might have been with a full moon.

George Bernard Shaw's brows were substantial, particularly during his later years, when they fairly swept skyward; and we are introduced, in Act IV of *Caesar and Cleopatra*, not only to a harp-playing slave girl, but to her master, who is, in Shaw's unusually applied words *'an old musician, with a lined face, prominent brows, white beard, moustache and eyebrows twisted and horned at the ends, and a consciously keen and pretentious expression'*

'Twisted and horned, at the ends?' A peripheral character and minor vision of the future, perhaps, for the, then, forty-two year old Shaw.

That Leonardo Da Vinci neglected to give his *Mona Lisa* eyebrows is widely accepted, but quite possibly not so. The apparent revelation

21

came, in 2007, courtesy of French engineer, Pascal Cotte, who used state-of-the-art scanning techniques, to detect what he considers to be a left brow. If he's correct, we might presume a reduction of her features was caused by poor restoration. But what, then, of that famous enigmatic smile? Were the clues we seek stolen, effectively, from us? The eyes, after all, are said to be windows, upon the soul; but if that's so, the chaperones above them surely have a major role, in amplifying their message.

I recall a monochrome photograph, by Lord Snowdon, of the author, Graham Greene. Rarely have I seen a more assertive expression. There he sits; starkly side-lit; a hand resting near his shoulder, with its index finger pointing to a spectacular and seemingly frosted left eyebrow. Snow may fall, upon Everest, but it's nothing compared with the winteriness there. His eyes send forth a stare that could fell a charging rhino, at fifty paces, while the right brow is forcefully cocked. Such mannerisms can have a certain come hither quality, at least, when exhibited by women, but, conversely, this seems to say, "clear off to Timbuktu and I don't mean tomorrow!" well, to me, anyway. Was it something the celebrated man of portraiture said?

With Marilyn Monroe, it's very different. In some images; most notably the work of Andy Warhol; she seems more inviting than a freshly-warmed and fluffed pillow; though one, of course, strictly for play; yet imagine that classic depiction, with the forehead unadorned. Certainly, she'd look pretty, but that, I suggest, is the point. Without the looping curves of her brows, she might have seemed merely attractive; instead, tilting the head back, whilst raising them, made her mesmerizing. Audrey Hepburn, in that same era, wore her brows prominently, too, although the elegance of her may make us blind to the fact. Those in doubt can visit stills, from *Breakfast at Tiffany's* and other movies, in which she starred. Carefully shaped they were, but nonetheless sumptuous and quite enough to provide an eminently satisfying double-bill.

Audrey had magnetism, but Hollywood has, perhaps, never exploited the wonders of the forehead more effectively than in Miramax's *Chicago*; Kander and Ebb's sinuous tale, in which Roxy Hart and Velma Kelly; two spectacularly feline females; seek to discard their murderous credentials and perform to the hoi polloi, atop the highest trash can in town; but, not without a swipe, or twenty, along the way. "Here's a message, straight from me to you. Keep your paws off my underwear!" declares Velma; her eyes delivering the 'or else' an instant before those lush, velvet, brows perform their leap of approval. "Thanks for nothing" comes Roxy's riposte; her left riser reaching for the rafters. It's an ongoing spat to be remembered; still more so when the advice dispensed is to stay off the caramels; and each, acerbic, rejoinder is, of course, accompanied by a shot, from the forehead. "He had it coming", we hear over and over, amid the *Cell Block Tango's* steamy spectacle and that may be so, but it surely wasn't the bullet that did for him; it was more likely the brow. *Chicago* is, of course, a tale of shocking injustice; with Renee Zellweger acting her rocks off, only to see Catherine Zeta Jones walk away with the Oscar. Even so, its makers raised a fair few dollars and that's not the half of it.

Mona Lisa's missing eyebrows have been the subject of much discussion, but let's not overlook a painting sometimes referred to as 'The Mona Lisa of the North', Johannes Vermeer's ever-enchanting *Girl with a Pearl Earring.* Brows she may have, but I wish you luck in your efforts to discern them; and it may be no coincidence that she, too, is often termed enigmatic.

Whether mopped, in accordance with a song you just might recall, or un-mopped, the brow of LS Lowry was well defined; at least, going by his own hand. In a self-portrait so starkly arresting it might engrave itself in our minds, he seems immersed in another world and crying, to us, from beyond an irremovable pane of glass. It may, then, not surprise you that he was, at that time, in a tight corner. His father had died, leaving behind a burden of debt, whilst his mother found herself unable to cope. And so Salford's celebrated artist shouldered a duty of care. Painting would take place, each evening, when she'd fallen asleep and continue throughout the night; as the blazing redness in his eyes appear to confirm.

A notable absence from Edvard Munch's most famous painting, *The Scream*, is difficult to explain. All three versions were, after all, full-on expressions of fear: so, if eyebrows convey anything, at all, we might well expect to see them. Perhaps though, there's a distinction to be made, because *The Scream* may not be, in the same sense, emotional. Rather than reacting to a specific occurrence;

bereavement, perhaps, or war; Munch's account relates, it seems, an inexplicable moment, of terror. Here's the story, as the artist told it:

"I was walking along a path, with two friends. The sun was setting. Suddenly, the sky turned blood red. I paused, feeling exhausted, and leaned on the fence. There was blood and tongues of fire above the blue-black fjord and the city. My friends walked on, and I stood there, trembling with anxiety; and I sensed an infinite scream passing through nature."

Banksy is believed to have his own, unique, take, on the revelatory properties of the brow; believing that policemen and security guards may wear low-peaked hats for psychological reasons. Eyebrows are, it's true, very expressive and people do appear more authoritative with them covered. "A possible advantage", the enigmatic graffiti-artist is reputed to have said, "is that it becomes more difficult for them to see anything more than six feet off the ground; which is why painting rooftops and bridges is so easy."

And in far-away Tokyo, the much maligned pioneer of plastination, Gunther Von Hagens was awakened, during the first of his 'Body

Worlds' exhibitions. Although 550,000 people attended, to see the German anatomist's assemblage of preserved corpses, no voices were raised, in protest. Some, though, did find them scary. The answer, Von Hagens quickly discovered, was to leave the eyebrows in place and use them to create a range of expressions. It seems the artist had overlooked the need for an indication of personality, or, at least, the best way to achieve it.

Like their tame relatives, lions do not have eyebrows; but zoological accuracy would prove no obstacle to the *Walt Disney Productions*, when creating *The Lion King*. They are dark, prominent and much utilized, even upon the young Simba. Disney did, in fact, cotton on to the power of the brow donkeys' years ago. In *The Jungle Book* (way back in 1967) we can see them on the faces of 'Sheer Khan' (a sinister tiger, you probably recall); an entire troop of marching elephants; Baloo (the clowning bear, who loved life's 'bare necessities'); King Louis (the priceless Orang -utan and 'jungle VIP') and even the vultures (searching for 'friends' of the edible kind). No opportunity is missed, to engage linearly, with the audience, to maximum effect.

There's the world of screen animals, but surely we would even less expect to see eyebrows upon railway engines; yet, as I've previously mentioned, Norman, the Diesel Engine and other friends of Thomas wore them. That said, perhaps anything goes when you're out of your shed; and of course, doubt may yet be cast upon the evolutionary aspect. If it's true, some might argue, that they were left in place, as hair coverage gradually receded, why does everyone's favourite caveman, Fred Flintstone, sport a pair of shapely and really quite delicate looking 'lady-brows'? Evolutionists will be untroubled by such a question, but creationists may well feel it strengthens their case.

And here's a question, for you. What's the best way to get out of the rain, in Polynesia? Well, shelter, of course, under the forehead of a giant! And it could just about be achieved, because the ancient statues on Easter Island are blessed with great protrusion; but, it's 'brow', in the TS Elliott sense, for they have nothing more. Known as *moai* and created between the thirteenth and sixteenth centuries, the figures stand in various sizes and reflect an ancient reverence toward the more chiefly head. Most are made of compressed volcanic ash (known as *tuff*), although a few were carved from trachyte; basalt, or scoria; and all are the creative antithesis of the delicate looking, smooth paddles, also associated with the region. Sometimes referred to as *rapas*, Easter Island paddles are rare and housed in some of the world's most prestigious museums; yet, the name is deceptive, for their purpose was usually ceremonial. With little timber available, they were carved from driftwood and offer an approximate, yet easily recognisable sense of the human form. At one end is a well-rounded abdomen, with a somewhat suggestive protrusion; put there, no doubt, for the embarrassment of museum curators; and at the other; connected by the most delicate looking of stems; sits a beautifully simplified head; arched, much like that of a lady in a veil, or a twentieth century milkmaid. All detail is absent, save for a small projection on each side, to indicate, perhaps, adorned ears and more obviously, the brow; curving in an M shape, to meet with a fine and vertical line, for the nose. Clearly, the island's inhabitants had exemplary taste!

Snow fell, copiously, upon the forehead of Karl Marx, if we believe the bust that rests upon his London grave, or maybe we're observing vast cumulous clouds, above the base of his nose. Whatever the truth, it can be difficult to accept we're seeing a pair of eyebrows; yet there they are, weighing heavily, above those dark, cavernous, eye-sockets. The actual appearance of Marx is known, although not well. His figurative final curtain having fallen in 1883, when photography was still in its infancy, we're left to inspect a gallery of low-quality shots and a surprisingly small number of paintings; mostly by lesser known artists. And so we might wonder whether the visual spectacle seen at Highgate is born, largely, of the sculptor's imagination. The beard, in almost all images, is sufficient to clean the sides of the Rotherhithe Tunnel, by way of a single walk-through visit, but his brows, in contrast, are quite slender. Are we then to conclude that the father of communism was an inveterate plucking revolutionary; at least, when sensing the imminent approach of a camera, or paintbrush? More likely, the creator of Highgate's posthumous tribute chose to invoke the brow and cause us to gaze, admiringly, upon an authoritative thinker, laudably bearing the weight of his own colossal imagination.

Muppet creator Jim Henson's scientifically laudable decision not to equip the bona fide superstar known as *Kermit the Frog* with eyebrows was, I suppose, the puppeteers' equivalent of choosing to cycle without use of the hands, but Henson was a master of his craft and well capable of saying it in other ways. Characters he gave brows tend to be somewhat aggressive and very large; yet *The Amazing Mumford*, a benign and level-headed magician, whose voice, incidentally, was based upon that of the comedian WC Fields, has nothing else, in the relevant region. Not, even, eyes. Henson and his team were, it's clear, prepared to take many a chance, in delivering their enduring style of magic.

We can only imagine the brows of photographer Don McCullin's shell-shocked Vietnam combatant, because they are concealed, within the grave-like cavern of his helmet; in a realm we would not wish to visit; and so we're left to ponder his stare, while those contorted fingers cage the prosthesis known as his gun. Maybe he's killed, or all but died; and though one may lead to the other, he stares on. He was made that way, by comfortable dignitaries, who smile at banquets and send young men to war; and might those objects of our frequent amusement be heavy with the detritus of bloody left and right? Sure as heck, they wouldn't dance, and though the brow is a messenger, his would tell us nothing. Only stand as a barrier we do not wish to see.

We may, then, choose to consider other, flaming, brows. Those shocked, from far above. Those whose owners cannot begin to comprehend the lousy failings of men. McCullin's broken soldier sickens; yet, our own furrowed features might well say better him than they.

Chapter 2 **Legends of the Brow**

It seems, to me, that today's screen-actors utilise their furry upper-regions less than those in the golden age of Hollywood; and if that's so, did their predecessors tend to overact, or is the modern way somewhat lacking? In the early years of talkies, bold mannerisms were, of course, to be expected. They had, after all, been saying it without words, for a long time; and significant changes, in style, do not occur overnight; yet there's great elegance in some of those scenes; and that fine tradition of upper-facial artistry continued at very least into the seventies. Step to it, then, present and future *007*s. If the language of the brow was good enough for Connery and Moore, it surely is for you!

With feathery right asset seated, commendably, upon a monocle; complete with chain, the sadly deceased astronomer, Sir Patrick Moore, was a true legend of the brow. That, surely, is the benchmark to which all should aspire, although few could carry the look, with

33

such panache. He was the superlative stargazer and a fine ambassador for optical adornment, but there are others to consider. We might look to the clergy; not for spiritual guidance, but because of their frequent wiriness and, in at least one case, extraordinary tonal quality. I'll spare my eminent candidate his blushes, but you could suspend half your Christmas decorations on each protrusion and how their darkness stands out, while framed by the silveriness of his crown and beard; indeed, it's rumoured that he's been sneaking into the whispering gallery of St. Paul's, to offer the somewhat optimistic request: "give us this day a bit more grey." In contrast, the celebrated atheist, Professor Richard Dawkins may be proud of his fine flares; and some would say he has more reason.

Other stand-out brow-wearers have a real touch of Groucho Marx about them and we might imagine the regular appearance, of their inky attributes, in Transport for London's lost property store. Further to that, Candida Lycett-Green; daughter of the late Poet Laureate, Sir John Betjeman; has, I understand, yet to see a man with darker eyebrows than the former Chancellor of the Exchequer, Alistair Darling. His high contrast visage caused her to speculate, in a way that, frankly, boggles the mind. She'd never seen a white bush, she declared. Those who served, with Darling, in Gordon Brown's cabinet, may feel more relief than curiosity.

Eyebrows are an impressionists' dream; and lest I be reminded that Claude Monet did not paint them, floating in his lake, I'm talking BBC prime-time here, throughout my days of youth. Without question, that great man of voices, Mike Yarwood, must have thought all his birthdays, Christmases and everything else, had come at once, when the gloriously endowed Chancellor of the Exchequer, Denis Healey entered number eleven; and hirsute history. The notable prominences of Alistair Darling might have curled with envy, because Denis sported a phenomenon more akin to loft insulation; and Yarwood grasped the opportunity, as might any other creditable tax-payer. Reaching for his admirable stick-ons, he made James Callaghan's chancellor one of his best loved personae; enabling him to pronounce Sir Keith Joseph, Enoch Powell, Ian Macleod and pretty much anyone else, on the Parliamentary scene, a "Silly Billy"

Somewhat confusingly, the actor Daniel Radcliffe has featured highly in polls, intended to establish both the sexiest eyebrows and the gnarliest; proving that, figuratively, most of us have at least a small quantity of Marmite upon our forehead; and it may also explain why I've heard so many Americans talk about '*Hairy Potter!*' Certainly, Lindy West, writing in The Telegraph, about Radcliffe's possible appearance in *All Quiet on The Western Front*, left little doubt about which camp she was in. Radcliffe was, to her, stiff, awkward, and unreasonably eyebrowed. The fashion magazines had said that a natural look was in, but his upper regions appeared to be taking over not just his face, but nearby townships, herds of livestock, passing hot air balloons, and small natural land masses. 'I can't wait to be wrong' she continued, 'just, please, can somebody trim his brows, before you send Radcliffe down into the trenches?'

With the world at his feet, Elvis clearly had it going on. While nervous television producers chewed their nails, in trepidation that his gyrating pelvis might be revealed, those hyperactive brows were sending mesmerised girls into orbit. Later in his career, they would be dyed, by his personal hairdresser, or so it's said; together with the lashes that lay beneath; but, by then, he was bigger than the universe, so really needn't have bothered. And if the late, great, songwriter Kirsty Maccoll was correct, you just might meet 'The King' in your local chip shop. It's a sobering thought and if you do, be sure to remind him that they did, indeed, love him tender and there are at least two reasons why.

With Sir Paul McCartney, it's different. His ease of eyebrow movement, particularly during those head-wobbling days, in the sixties, suggests there may be some form of invisible mechanism, upon which they swing. All other explanations seems, to me, implausible, because I've practiced eight days a week and still can't work it out.

Sir Roger Moore was self-deprecating, when critics went for the forehead. He'd never thought himself much of an actor, he once said and that his acting range had always been between the two extremes. Those of 'raises left eyebrow' and 'raises right eyebrow'. Clearly, he was a modest man and his many fans would insist there was a great deal more to it than that. And fellow actor Christian Slater, has admitted growing tired of comparisons. "If I raise my eyebrows, people say I'm doing Nicholson", he has complained; and asked whether he's supposed to cut his eyebrows off.

At this point, I feel compelled to express a preference, because there's one look I've long found unappealing. Why on earth a healthy and otherwise attractive woman would pluck her eyebrows away and replace them with straight black lines, more suited to an androgynous stick-figure, remains, to me, a mystery. It is, however, merely a personal view; so, if the eyes that scan this page sit beneath the said arrangement, please don't take offence. You may love your chosen look, as might your partner; but, to me, it's as pleasing as a bluebottle on a Monet, or a garish hula-hoop around the moon. Nevertheless, some have accentuated the concept, to spectacular effect. I refer, almost exclusively, to the long-departed silent-movie star, Clara Bow. Her public manifestation would be, for sheer impact, difficult to surpass and it's easy to see, in stills, how those wilting arcs relentlessly thrust forth her melancholic eyes, in ways that would be impossible to ignore; the effect being still more arresting, when beneath a head-scarf, or brimless hat. Clara was very much the party girl, with, according to her assistant, Daisy Devoe, a libido that just wouldn't stop and gained a consequent reputation for promiscuity. The look and the lifestyle may, though, not be difficult to explain. Born in Brooklyn, to a mentally ill mother and rejecting father, a subsequent yearning for attention seems quite logical. Despite the resulting lull in her career, she did return to the silver screen; in the movies *Call Her Savage* (1932) and *Hoopla* (1933). But, her public image remained tainted. Many years after her death, a biography, entitled *Running Wild*, was written, by David Stenn; in which he attempted to clarify her story. Clara's own words may, though, say it best: "All the time the flapper is laughin' and dancin', there's a feelin' of tragedy underneath…"

Clara's brows swept south, like the drowsy wings of an owl. Not so with Twiggy, whose doe eyes were carried to us by a spirited seagull, albeit a dusky one; as were those of Jean Shrimpton; yet, Simon Hattenstone, of *The Guardian* was keen, in 2002, to inform readers of Jean's former fiancé, the photographer David Bailey's tousled mops. His eyebrows, Hattenstone said, could be used for fusewire and he would, at that time, have made a good King Lear; and further to that, Brad Darrach, writing for *People* magazine, noted the young Olivier's "huge black eyebrows, that met in the middle and hung, like an awning, over both of his eyes; making him look more like Caliban than Hamlet." A barber took care of the cosmetic problems, he suggested; and talent did the rest.

Barry Humphreys' gloriously vulgar creation, Sir Les Patterson, warrants a mention, too. Few may have the relevant tactile knowledge, but it's easy to imagine their coarseness and he's probably trying to devise a method of throwing up in them, as I write.

Should we wish to find a Mexican icon, of the brow, we need search no further than the late great, artist, Frida Kahlo. The seminal moment came in her eighteenth year, when she ditched the nail scissors and chose to let two become one. She would, then, forever be associated with the most spectacular and commendable of mono-brows. As her fellow artist and husband, Diego Rivera, observed, it "perched on her brow (again, in the sense of TS Elliott) like a blackbird's outspread wings." It's more than a touch poetic, and ornithologically pretty sound.

If the brow of Frida Kahlo was well compared with a blackbird, then Bob Monkhouse's hovered, like a melanistic kestrel; "Willie, dear Willie Rushton" he'd say, whilst gazing toward an array of celebrities, surely held captive; and as he did, his would seem to flutter, in anticipation of a witticism. When he improvised, they would steady and one could sense the cogs powering his thought. "Growing old is compulsory", he once declared, "growing up is optional." A celebrity himself and clearly no square, Monkhouse was essential to brow culture, like Elvis, to the pelvis.

Spotting Isambard Kingdom Brunel, on London's Embankment, may seem surprising, more than a hundred and fifty years after his death; but less so when he's cast in bronze. Baron Marochetti's statue inhabits the corner of Temple Place and is well elevated. Perhaps the greatest engineer born of our isles, he stands, in deep contemplation and it would be near-sacrilegious to say that a percussion ensemble could play upon his substantial forehead. His stance is informal; a hands in pockets posture; although, in fact,

41

they're not. He could, instead, almost be peeling potatoes. Beneath his well-fitting coat, the top of his waistcoat is casually unbuttoned and his boots may have been bought in nearby Carnaby Street. He has mutton chops and a look of intensity; his left brow kept low; with the right raised, to spectacular effect. Believe them, if you must, when they tell you he's clutching his drawing implement, whilst scrutinising one of his ships, or bridges. He created the Great Western Railway and stands, at the terminus, staring along half a mile of shining steel. He's ripped his ticket in two and will surely swear, as he turns to leave: "How many years did I toil, to give our nation this wonder, and then they can't be bothered to make the bloody trains run on time?!"

The chalk giant at Cerne Abbas has eyebrows, although you may not have noticed them. Best known for his, well, let's just say prominence, within the Dorset landscape and believed to have been created around four hundred years ago, he appears more primitive than that and wears, in addition to absolutely nothing, an expression of puzzlement; the brows raised, as though he's wondering what the fuss is about. He is a crude representation. A neither sweet nor savoury ginger-bread man, thrust before the public gaze, whether we like it or not. The club he brandishes can easily be envisaged bouncing, comically, from his disproportionately small head; as he repeatedly attempts to knock himself unconscious; perhaps for having forgotten his underwear; and his feet are in disagreement with the rest of his body. And yet, we cherish him, as he is. In America, they'd, likely as not, cover his extension, with 'Old Glory' and croon *The Star Spangled Banner;* before dinging a bell. But, here, in fair England, we'd sooner risk offending our grandmothers, for the sake of heritage, whether it's noble or not. He's usually viewed from the nearby road; the National Trust restricting access to the hillside; but despicable rule-breakers can make the climb and perch upon his forehead. We might, though, presume, that, being somewhat distracted, few do.

We may laugh, in ignorance, at the giant, and perhaps even at Brunel, but the ancient battle-helmet, unearthed at Sutton Hoo, demands serious attention. Pieced together, from hundreds of tiny fragments, it almost sings, through the ages, in its primal artistry. Like the face of some baleful, perhaps unearthly, insect, it calls us to journey back in time, via the blackness of its interior, to its creation, in the seventh century; yet, we might prefer to linger a while and absorb its finery. Central to the visage; at the base of the nose, is the semblance of a dragon's head, linking with the golden crest; which bisects the domed crown. The nose, itself, extends, as a single plate, to meet with the upper lip, which could be interpreted, through our twenty-first century eyes, as a neatly trimmed moustache. All very impressive; and I'm delighted to confirm that eyebrows were not omitted. They fan away, toward each side, like plumes, inlaid with silver wire and garnets; and at the end of each, is a small gilded head; seemingly, that of a boar. The helmet's detail may be mesmerising, but, to get the full picture, take a few steps back. You may, then, see its elements combine, to resemble an ornate bird, in flight: with the brows forming the glinting falcon-like wings. And so, a rusted, though fascinating, artefact reveals itself to be a work, not only of beauty, but great imagination.

Meanwhile, in a galaxy far, far, away there sat a jazzed-up version of the Suffolk helmet, upon a long- cloaked tyrant; known, to *Odeon* dwellers, as Darth Vader. The man inside was Dave Prowse; a west country actor and body-builder, required to cast aside his recitations of the green-cross-code and we might assume, keep it firmly zipped, while American, James Earl Jones voiced the part, without so much as a hint of *The Wurzels*. Prowse was, of course, magnificent; allowing the action sequences to thrill and audience members, in turn, to spill their popcorn; yet the grand unmasking; in *Return of the Jedi*, would reveal the face of Shakespearean actor, Sebastian Shaw. Grey as stone and sunken-eyed; he pleads, silently, for our sympathy and despite his dark ways, gets it. He is egg-shaped. Broken on top; and with eyebrows digitally removed, for the *DVD* version, appeals more to our better nature than before. He has fallen from his wall. He is Humpty Dumpty. Shaw speaks, for less than a minute, before being laid to rest, but his performance is captivating. In reality, his final breath came eleven years later. It was the end of a long and distinguished career, in which the actor played numerous major roles; including King Lear; Polonius, in *Hamlet*; Hal, in *Henry IV* and numerous others. Most famously, though, he was the last vestige of Anakin Skywalker; the Jedi knight, who became *Vader*; lost his eyebrows and then his life. They were expunged, incidentally, for plot consistency; young Anakin's features having, in the *Revenge of the Sith* prequel, been spectacularly burned.

Back on the planet we call home, appointing a 'King of the Brow' can never be easy. There are, of course, many to choose from and you will surely have your own; based in part, perhaps, on the individual's sex-appeal; but I'm interested in something other; so should I look to legends such as Sir Patrick Moore, his namesake Roger; or the celebrated wearer, Denis Healey? Well, not necessarily; because there's at least one modern politician to consider: a man with eyebrows that lift, like flappers, on a pinball machine and might cause us to ponder when we last witnessed the opening of Tower Bridge. A likely candidate, he will long direct us north of the border; yet I'll veer in a different direction and journey through history.

Former Soviet President Leonid Brezhnev's lower forehead was perilous, to both man and beast; not least because large areas of it never, perhaps, saw daylight. Maps were drawn and search parties dispatched, for the benefit of explorers, who'd become lost and disorientated; when attempting to journey from east to west. I do, of course, exaggerate; very slightly. Younger readers, not privileged to have viewed that unwelcoming bear of a man, as he stood there epitomising the expression 'death warmed up'; while his collection of soldiers high kicked, below, are advised to seek a photograph and perhaps draw a picture. Those with a pen would, though, be well advised to check their supply of ink. It must, then, be a posthumous coronation, because only he can truly be declared King of the Brow.

Selecting a Queen is more difficult; because the options are fewer. Off-the-wall eyebrows are almost not existent among the fairer sex, so it is, inevitably, much more a contest of allure. Here, then, are a few we might consider: Vivien Leigh (of course); Penelope Cruz (arguably, the new Audrey); Frida Kahlo (the closest, perhaps, we'll find to wild); or Marilyn Monroe (captivating and submissive).

This time, though, I'm going for someone previously unmentioned, within these pages: a resplendent musician; and how beautifully those expressive wonders rose and fell, as she sang, in the seventies, of her beloved Wuthering Heights. Beguiling, idiosyncratic and many a discerning schoolboy's dream; she has yet to be equalled. There really is only one Kate Bush.

Well, those are my King and Queen, but you will surely have your own. Choose them well, fellow brow fans; and don't let their crowns slip too low!

Chapter 3   The Rise and the Fall of It

Irrespective of eyebrows' usefulness, those who do ask why we were given them would, I suggest, be well advised to reconsider their question. That's because what facial coverage we own has, instead, been retained, through process of evolution. It's a subtle distinction, but, nonetheless, one that many reasoned thinkers hold dear. The question, then, of why so few of our fellow mammals have eyebrows can easily be answered: it's because holding on to their fuller coverage has benefitted their species. Looking through a book's index one could easily be misled; less so among mammals; although there does exist a rather splendid 'White-browed Gibbon' which sports striking eyebrow-like markings; but 'browed' birds are all over the place. There are Yellow browed Warblers; White-browed Robin Chats; Black-browed Albatrosses (actually more of a dark grey smudge, but let's not be pedantic); Turquoise-browed Motmots;

49

White-browed Coucals (an African cuckoo); Fiery-browed Mynah's (let's hope it's not reflected in their language!); White-browed Wagtails; the more explicitly named Eye-browed Thrush and many more. An impressive selection, you might think, but in point of fact, none of those mentioned possesses anything which approximates to a real brow; they merely have differently coloured clumps of feathers, above their eyes; usually forming stripes, known as a 'supercilia'. Still more confusingly, birds that do possess something more closely comparable tend not to be nominally recognised for doing so. They include some species of owl; with their bristly feathering, extending back from the bill (although it's arguable that Tawny-browed and White-browed Hawk Owls are exceptions); game birds, such as Grouse, which sport red comb-like features; used for display, rather than protective purposes (during my research, I was interested to discover that those with larger ones are far more likely to be polygamous) and some species of penguin; which possess lavish ornamental quills.

The adjective, supercilious, incidentally, is derived from the Latin *supercilium*; which means eyebrow. It describes, according to the

Oxford English Dictionary, someone with an 'air of contemptuous superiority' and relates, many believe, to gratuitous raising of the brow. In its unaltered form, supercilium remains in common usage; although, almost exclusively, among ornithologists; to describe the aforementioned stripe.

Of course, some mammals; most notably, camels; do possess a significant thickening, of fur, above their eyes; including a few breeds of dog; and high, on the list, should feature the Scottish Terrier. Less likely than others to endanger families, in the park; they are old looking, even when young, ought to smell of whisky; and for reasons, I think, other than their Scottishness, tend to remind me of the motor-racing champion, Sir Jackie Stewart. Something which, I hasten to add, , may have a great deal more to do with me than with him. In addition, rumour has it that, unlike the human population of that fair land, they really do occasionally say "och hay the noo!"; so it just might be worth tracking one down, on Burns night, for the sheer entertainment of it; if, that is, you haven't got other things to do; such as spending time with your cat.

I would not wish to write, authoritatively, about matters of the body and mind; or much else, for that matter. This is, after all, a voyage, of discovery, for both you and me; yet, by way of my research, I discovered many snippets of information I found fascinating, so I'm pleased to play the expert and share them with you:

Eyebrow movement requires the use of two muscles; called the *frontalis* and the *corrugator;* the former raises the brow and the latter can produce a frown.

Although some find it difficult to cock just one eyebrow, those who have overcome their apparent inability to emulate Elvis may confirm that it can achieved, through muscle-training. Even so, why would it be significantly more difficult for some than for others? Well, quite simply because we don't all have the same equipment. The examination of cadavers has revealed that facial musculature varies, considerably; all of us possessing the five, core, muscles, but only some having the others required, for ease of movement. Those without the full set need not, though, be disheartened. It's really just a matter of training alternative ones to do the job, instead.

Two systems, in the brain, control the facial muscles: the emotional and the volitional. Research indicates that the more emotional expressions, which tend to involve both sides of the face, are controlled by areas such as the *supplementary motor cortex* and *rostral cingulated gyrus*, while volitional movement (non-spontaneous expression) is dependent on alternative routes that serve only one side. These include the *primary motor cortex* and the *caudal cingulated gyrus*. It's a highly sophisticated set-up, although with a degree of variation; and geared more to the lower regions of the face than the upper; so, not, for everyone, an instant brow raiser.

The role, of eyebrows, in facial recognition, should not be underestimated. Volunteers were asked, to identify a series of well-known faces; ranging from former US presidents, to movie stars; all of them minus either their eyes or their eyebrows. The results may surprise you. The recognition rate, relating to images void of eyes, was sixty per cent. For those without eyebrows, the figure was a mere forty-six. Clearly, then, brows are important, for purpose of identification, but, the way they reveal our thoughts is less so. I've seen mention that the single, raised, eyebrow is a universal sign of scepticism, but did the extraordinary allure of Brigitte Bardot, in her heyday, have much to do with that? Consider, too nineteen-seventies dance troupes, such as *Hot Gossip* and Benny Hill's distinctly saucy *Hill's Angels*. There, amid the skimpy outfits, suggestive movements and enticing glances, one-sided raising could be seen; and to borrow from Anne Bancroft's Mrs Robinson, when attempting to ensnare Dustin Hoffman, they more conveyed the question "would you like me to seduce you?" than "you'd rather be watching the football, wouldn't you?"

They are, of course, small illustrations. Even so, those concerned held, it seems, little doubt that a raised eyebrow could help to drive the message home; so, while I don't wish to be over sceptical about scepticism, there is, I suspect, a fair bit more to it.

Of one thing I am, though, completely convinced. That the brow can be an emphasiser of what's within our eyes; amplifying all they need to say; and where, then, does that leave cancer patients? Hair loss, as you will surely know, occurs during chemotherapy and not just from the top of the head; so, we'd all be well advised to make special allowance, for their diminished ability to communicate. Because, an aid to connecting is lost.

The dual raised eyebrow is widely thought to be a sign of surprise; yet, I've previously suggested that, where Marilyn Monroe is concerned, it appears to have more to do with submission; and we are, of course, living in an age of neurotoxins, when a shot too far can leave one interminably resembling Kenneth Williams' Caesar, when he finally realised they'd all got it in for him; so, it really has all become a bit hazy.

There are, of course, rooms in which body language has no place; for, justice is not born of mannerisms; yet, some studies indicate that dishonest individuals experience difficulty, in suppressing their eyebrow movements. We might place, beside them, those who do not.

It's said, too, that other tendencies exist; that spontaneous expressions are symmetrical and those we affect, less so. Animators, anyway, like to initiate brow movement, in advance of their creation's head and lower-body. Doing so evokes thought and further emphasises the nature of each scene.

Back in the real world, we might notice the way brows tend to rise, with the pitch of their owner's voice and fall again, as it lowers; and that, when they are asking a genuinely investigative question, they are low; but when the answer is already known, high.

Further to that, anyone with faith in physiognomy may be aware that, while straight eyebrows tell us someone is active and in control; but, with a tendency to be negligent of detail; gently curved ones indicate balance and self- awareness. Arches, on the other hand (not true ones, which would, of course, constitute a first for science) suggest not only a sense of curiosity, but a lack of trust, with regard to relationships; and then there are widely spaced ones, which tell us someone is easily influenced. Those who can be bothered with such pseudo-scientific nonsense should also be told that large ear lobes indicate potential prosperity, a down-turned mouth, obstinacy and that, in history, many a poor sod will have been executed, as a direct consequence of their physical characteristics. Anyway, moving swiftly on…

When eyebrows sit lower on the face than is usual, the condition is known as *ptosis*. It arises, most often, from gravitational and involutional (the shrinkage of organs in old age) changes within the body, although there can be other causes, including tumors; facial palsy and asymmetry, produced by trauma. Fortunately, many forms of brow-lifting surgery are now available.

The normal procedure for removing a brain-tumour is known as a craniotomy. An unenviable task, we might imagine, it involves the removal of skin and opening of the skull; so the risks of facial scarring and excessive blood loss, together with that of infection, would usually be high. Use of the eyebrow method, has helped, though. The process involves entering the body, at the eyebrow, in order to access the base of the skull. Minimal scarring results, together with reduced loss of bodily fluids and any risk of infection, particularly by meningitis.

The piercing of eyebrows, merely for decoration, has become very popular, although research indicates an element, of risk. Within a bone that lies behind the eyebrow, can be found a small notch, known as the *supraorbital foramen*, which contains the supraorbital vein and nerve. Both are shielded, by the surrounding bone channel, piercing of which could result in nerve damage. It may take an eminently cack-handed operative to perforate both the bone and skin. Even so, those wishing to undergo the procedure might be well advised to steer clear of Mr Bean types.

In the beginning was not the brow; yet religious leaders have had
much to say about the treatment of them. Some, within Islam, insist
that plucking is forbidden and that those who have done so are
cursed. Sikhs, too, are advised not to reach for the tweezers; but
Christians are permitted to pluck away, until the proverbial cows
come home, although the piercing, of eyebrows, is sometimes
opposed. For that, they can thank a catchy little quote, from
Leviticus:

*"Ye shall not make any cuttings in your flesh, nor print any marks
upon you: I am the Lord"*

That's telling them. Presumably, then, the safety-pins at concerts by
the Sex Pistols will have crossed the line. They were, it seems, a
band intent on sinking the boat, yet you had to be a fan; if you

wanted to arrive home without phlegm on your jacket; or, for that matter, with it. Anyway, in those volatile climes, the monarch's upper reaches were spared; artist Jamie Reid having chosen to pierce her disputably majestic lips, instead, in his promotional artwork for *God Save the Queen*.

In Hinduism, the region between the eyebrows; the sixth *chakra*; is said to house concealed wisdom; and the familiar *tilak* ; also known as *tilaka* or *bindi*; is worn there, for retentive reasons. Where women are concerned, it takes the form of a small dot, of varying colour; and placement, at what is believed to be an exit point, is said to retain *kundalini* energy. Furthermore, it's believed to ward away demons and bad luck.

On males, the statement is a fair bit bolder and comes in the form of a series of coloured lines, reaching from hairline to eyebrows. The purpose differs too. They indicate the possibility of good luck and when worn by females, wedlock.

Although sported, by *sadhus* and pious citizens, on a daily basis, Hindus tend to reserve the tilak for significant occasions, including weddings and religious ceremonies. In addition, they are applied, by priests, to indicate a blessing. Placed by hand, or a metal stamp, tilaks are formed from a broad range of ingredients; including charcoal, clay, turmeric, cow dung, sandalwood paste and ash; sometimes from a sacrificial fire; and are said to cool the forehead and aid concentration. Where symbolism is concerned, tilaks worn between the eyebrows reference the third eye of Lord Shiva; and those with absolute devotion (known as *Saivites*) wear, specifically, three horizontal lines, with the dot sometimes absent, and sometimes, a crescent moon, or trident, in its place.

With *Vaishnavites* (those who follow *Vishnu*) the process differs, again; requiring the application of two vertical lines; made from sandalwood paste and joined together, to form a letter U (which suggests the foot of Vishnu), together, sometimes, with a central line, or the more familiar dot.

Overall, then, it's a complex affair, made still more so by women of other faiths, who wear the tilaka purely for aesthetic reasons. They can even be seen, occasionally, upon children; an erosion, perhaps, of traditional ways, or the emergence of a wear what you please society.

Also in Hinduism, Kali is the deity associated with destruction. She is dark skinned, possesses four arms, and wears a necklace of skulls; together with a girdle of hands, removed from giants she has slain. Not everyone's type then, particularly when her eyebrows stream red, with blood from her victims…and she carries around a human head and sword; yet goats are sacrificed, to her; and it's said that quite a few people have been, too.

Mongol emperor and founder of the Yuan dynasty, Kublai Khan, is said to have been greatly inspired by *Mahakala*; a deity who derives from *Bhairava*; the Hindu god, Shiva, in his fiercest manifestation; and if Tibetan iconography is believed, he was another extraordinary looking individual. Typically, he is depicted with three bulging eyes; their brows literally aflame; a beard, comprised of hooks; and six arms. Overall, not someone we'd ask the time of, despite his fetchingly fiery fashion-statement. Blazing eyebrows have, though, not been unique, to Mahakala. Olmecs dreamt of a divine dragon who possessed them; together with a bulbous nose and deeply forked tongue.

The history of humanity is, of course, bizarre, so it may not surprise you that ancient Egyptians were required to shave off their own eyebrows, upon the demise of their dear moggie; when, that is, they weren't consecrating their children to the cat god, *Bastet*, by introducing feline blood to their veins.

Were we to journey through ancient Egypt, we might encounter *the Eye of Horus*. Not the unwanted attention of some 'peeping tom', but a stylised representation of an eye, with its brow; often in the form of an amulet. More often referred to as *udjat;* the organ resembles a human one, but adorned with markings we'd see upon a falcon. Horus, the Egyptian sky-god, was associated with war and protection. Mythology tells us he fought with *Seth*, in attempting to avenge the death of his father and amidst the struggle, lost his left optic; an object known, to you and me, as the moon. Much time would elapse, before the corresponding god of wisdom and magic, *Thoth*, discovered its fragments and successfully pieced them together; ensuring that, more than seven thousand years later, astronaut Alan Shepard would have somewhere interesting to play golf.

Born of an ancient-Egyptian tendency to revere parents, udjat amulets would often be laid at their graves, to serve as substitutes for expected offerings; sort of an unusable IOU, though with proclaimed healing and resurrectional capabilities. More intimately, they would be placed amid dressings applied to mummies; immediately above incisions points; the body's internal organs having been removed. Doing so was thought to provide protection, in the afterlife, from the misfortune such extractions might, in their belief, otherwise have brought.

Ancient Persian culture had its gaze set firmly on the eye, too; together, of course, with the brow. Rumi's *Mathnawi* tells a tale of admonishment. That, in Umar's time, people ran, when the month of fast came round, to a hill-top. Their hope was to see the new moon. "Look!" said one, to Umar, "there is the new moon!" But Umar could not see the object and declared the sight had been born of his companion's imagination. "Otherwise", he continued, "since I am a better observer of the heavens than you are, why do I not see the pure crescent?" Umar advised that he wet his hand and rub his eyebrow, before looking again and having done so, the companion said, to Umar "Oh king! There is no moon. It has disappeared." "Yes", Umar replied, "the hair from your eyebrow became a bow and shot, at thee, an arrow of false opinion." A single displaced hair had caused him to boast that he'd seen the moon.

The story exists, I assume, to foster faith in the 'righteous'. That one can only be sure of seeing clearly with their guidance; alluded to, as expertise, in eyebrow care.

…and in Chinese folklore, this barely edifying yarn can be found:

'Wei Gu, of the Tang dynasty, took a trip, to the city of Sung. In the evening, he came upon an old man, leaning against a large cloth bag and reading a big, thick book. He asked the old man what book he was reading, and the old man replied, "this book records marriages. I need only use one of the red ropes in this bag to tie a man's foot to a woman's and the two are sure to become man and wife." Then the old man stood up and began walking toward the rice market,

followed by Wei Gu. The old man pointed to a small girl, who was being carried by an old woman and said, "this is your future wife." Wei Gu grew very angry, wondering how this silly little girl could ever possibly be his wife and ordered his servant to kill her. But the servant merely made a small cut between the girl's eyebrows.

Fourteen years later, the provincial governor gave his daughter to Wei Gu, as a wife. The bride was extremely beautiful, except that she had a scar between her eyebrows. It was said that it had been made fourteen years earlier, when she was passing by the rice market, in the city of Sung, with her nanny. Upon hearing this Wei Gu finally believed what the old man had said.

Today, 'the old man under the moon' can refer to anyone who assumes the role of matchmaker.

In Norse mythology, when Odin killed *Ymir*, his body was used to create the world. His flesh, for the earth, His bones for mountains, His hair made into trees, His teeth boulders, His skull the sky and his brains into clouds. Humanity would be preserved, by way of a mighty wall, formed from his eyebrows; which surrounded a domain known as *Midgard.*

And in far-south New Zealand, *pikao*; or golden sand-sedge; carries great cultural significance. Prized as a weaving material, significant efforts have been made to conserve the plant. For Maoris, though, its meaning is more than functional. The story goes that, when the universe began, a great conflict formed, between the god of the forest; *Tane Mahuta* and his brother, *Takaroa* (of the sea). Jealous of Tane Mahuta's success, in separating father of the sky, *Ranginui* from mother of the earth, *Papa-tu-a-nuku,* Takaroa had warred against him. In his attempt to peacefully resolve their conflict, Tane Mahuta plucked his own eyebrows and presented them to Takaroa, as a token of friendship; yet Takaroa's feelings of envy were so overwhelming that he dismissively threw them to the shore. There they took root and continue to grow, as the Pikao plant; dividing forest and sea. The two brothers, it is said, battle on, to this day.

In addition to their deities, Incas held sacred a wide variety of locations, within their empire; those being known as *huacas.* Caves were given huaca status, along with mountain-tops, springs, quarries, battle-fields and caves. As villages were conquered, such areas would be ascribed specialness and were readily accepted, as so, by the Andean people. With reverence, men would sprinkle cocoa leaves, when passing a huaca, or place a stone, nearby; and such regions became easily identifiable, due to the resulting accumulations. Those who could offer neither would, instead, pluck hairs, from their eyebrows and blow them toward the relevant sacred area.

Chapter 5   **Issues of the Brow**

The term 'highbrow' entered popular usage, in the early twentieth

century, courtesy of Will Irvin, a newspaper journalist, working for

The Sun. He promoted the phrenological notion that intelligence is

revealed by the size of the forehead. Larger meant brighter;

presumably to contain all of those groundbreaking, genius, thoughts.

Now, of course, it has more of a cultural meaning; highbrow being

used to describe activities and forms of entertainment that are

presumed incomprehensible to the mere 'common' citizen. In short,

it's about social exclusion and sometimes inverted snobbery. The

nonsense of that mindset has been brought to light, every now and

then; most memorably during celebrations for the 1990 football

world cup, when Pavarotti expressed a liking for the game,

spectacularly emptied his balloons, before the multitude, and had

copies of Puccini's *Nessun Dorma* flying from the shelves, faster than a choral assemblage can chant off-side. Anyway, I digress, but that is where it comes from. It's about having high eyebrows.

References to the late American cartoonist Tad Dorgan as 'the cat's pyjamas' may, or may not, describe him; depending, I suppose, on opinions of his work. They would, though, be apt, because it was he who, in 1920, coined the expression. There are others, too, with which Dorgan is associated, including 'hot dog' (in case anyone's reading these words on some other planet, it refers to a sausage, shoved, unceremoniously, amid a bread roll), although many dispute that he thought of it first. About 'the flea's eyebrows', however, there's can be little doubt. Though rarely heard, these days, the expression was a fairly popular, throughout much of the twentieth century and carries the same meaning as the bee's knees, or more recently, the dog's bollocks (might I be permitted to introduce the pioneer of that phrase to the wonders of astronomy?); all of them referring, we are told, to something of excellence. Why the flea's hypothetical eyebrows, or any other questionable delights are considered superior to, let's say, the wing of a butterfly is anyone's guess. Nonetheless, true browologists really should be furnished with all detail.

I've mentioned that the ageing George Bernard Shaw's mops were substantial and I restate the fact, in order to steer my ramblings toward the 'Pygmalion effect'. Also known as the self-fulfilling prophecy, the theory proposes that belief greatly influences outcome. For example, if members of a football team believe, unanimously, that they are going to perform well, then, according to the theory, that's what will surely happen. An unusual case occurred, in 1911 and involved a horse, named Hans, who had an apparent propensity to perform mental arithmetic. The truth, though, was less remarkable, because Hans had merely been guided by the raising of his examiner's eyebrows; stamping his hoof, until his human companion, inadvertently, reacted to his arrival, at the correct number. Thus Hans had responded, repeatedly, to the manifestation of a belief that the task would be successfully performed. There are no great miracles, then, to report; only a further testament to the awesome power of the brow.

He was, I imagine, a stable lad, but long-serving Eton headmaster,

Dr. John Keate; said to have copiously lashed backsides, at that

loftiest of schools, between the years 1809 and 1834, would become

a figure of fun. That was due, in no small part, to his appearance;

and the historian Alexander Kinglake, who studied under him,

informs us that Dr Keate possessed a good deal other than his roving

right arm: 'He was little more; if more at all; than five feet, in height

and was not very great in girth, but within this space was

concentrated the pluck of ten battalions. You could not put him out

of humour; that is out of the ill-humour which he thought to be

fitting, for a Head Master. His red, shaggy eyebrows were so

prominent that he habitually used them as arms and hands, for the

purpose of pointing out any object towards which he wished to direct

others' attention."

More inspiringly, following the onset of his illness and prior to

receiving his speech- synthesizer, Professor Stephen Hawking could

communicate only by raising his eyebrows, as someone reached the

relevant letter, upon a card. He would go on to deliver such pertinent

observations as "I have noticed even people who claim everything is predestined and that we can do nothing to change it, look before they cross the road" and "The greatest enemy of knowledge is not ignorance, it is the illusion of knowledge." Sadly departed, he was a true champion of science and reason.

Sacred scripture may not describe the Virgin Mary's physicality, but that didn't prevent the blessed Mary of Agreda from giving it a go. Displaying the supreme insight of a celestial window-cleaner, she was quite specific. Here's her account, from *The Mystical City of God*:

'The bodily shape, of the heavenly Queen, was well proportioned and taller than is usual, with other maidens of her age; yet extremely elegant and perfect, in all its parts. Her face was rather more oblong than round, gracious and beautiful, without leanness or grossness; its complexion clear, yet of a slightly brownish hue; her forehead spacious yet, symmetrical; her eyebrows perfectly arched; her eyes large and serious, of incredible and ineffable beauty and dovelike sweetness, dark in colour, with a mixture tending toward green; her nose straight and well-shaped; her mouth small, with red-coloured lips, neither too thin nor too thick. All the gifts of nature in her were

73

*so symmetrical and beautiful, that no other human being ever had
the like'*

…and Anne Catherine Emmerich was similarly attentive to detail, in
The Life of Jesus Christ and Biblical Revelations:

*'The Blessed Virgin had auburn hair, dark eyebrows, fine and
arched, a very high forehead, large downcast eyes with long, dark,
lashes, a straight nose, delicate and rather long, a lovely mouth,
around which played a most noble expression, and a pointed chin.'*

Perish that someone so exemplary might have been less than
symmetrical, or worn them ragged.

Back in the larger world, we might further understand the emotional
connection that eyebrows offer, through studying the great violinists.
Not, merely, listening, to recordings, but watching their facial
movements, as they play. For me, seeing the creative process written
upon the face of Maxim Vengerov, or Chloe Hanslip enhances my
understanding of their artistry; and central to that is the brow. Should
you have access to relevant video recordings, try comparing your
experience with mine. The effect may be universal.

Consider, too, moments spent under the dentist's much loved drill. As our dearest pal wields his, or her, steel and attempts to reach the earth's core, via our root canals, are we not responsive, with our eyebrows? Wail we might, as an unsleeping nerve is angered, but we instinctively try to show our disapproval, in other ways. The gesture is, though, futile. The goggles forced upon us, these days, ensure that.

Anyway, music journalist, Ariane Toades, left little doubt about the focus of her attention. When viewing a 3D recording, of the Berlin Philharmonic Orchestra, she found herself greatly impressed and not just with their performance; or conductor Sir Simon Rattle's movement of the baton. Writing in *The Strad,* she observed that he shuts his eyes, as he listens and then raises one eyebrow and springs an eye open, to signify some musical moment. Who, she asked, needs cartoon flamingos, like in *Fantasia*, when you can watch Rattle's eyebrows?

This form of communication, among musicians, seems prevalent. Billy Cox; bass guitarist with Jimi Hendrix, during his time in the *Band of Gypsies,* has spoken, explicitly, about their method, for holding a performance together. They took their cues from Jimi. They could tell when his solos were going to end, by watching his eyebrows.

And *Mothers of Invention* front-man, Frank Zappa had an interesting take on modern technology; pointing out that computers can't tell the emotional story. They can give you the exact mathematical design, but what's missing is the eyebrows.

His creatively versatile daughter Moon Unit continues, in his footsteps.

Spare a thought, too, for the 'air guitarist'. How exposed is he?! Page, Knopfler and The Edge have at least a string-bearing slab of coated wood to fall back on, should their eyebrows fail to convey the message. He, on the other hand, stands there, naked, to the world. His endeavour is mind-boggling. Far too daunting for ordinary earthlings; yet perform he will. Throw his heart and soul to the chattering clientele of *The Mad Plucker's Arms*, in his attempt to convince them that *The Hotel California* really is, unequivocally, a lovely place. He is a communicator. We know him. We understand him. We spill a broad spectrum of beverages upon him; and all for one reason. Because he made a noble choice. For his trusted means of expression, he chose the brow.

On a different level, few would deny that Richard Wagner wrote music to stir the senses. For better or worse, that was surely his mission; but, we might note his apparent conceitedness. The parrot he owned would, it's said, screech "Richard Wagner, you're a great man" and when he plucked his eyebrows, his wife, Cosima, would keep each and every hair.

Rather than plucking them, *Peter Pan* author, JM Barrie, was a great wiggler of not only his eyebrows, but, his ears; those abilities providing frequent entertainment, for the Llewelyn Davies family. Readers familiar with the movie *Finding Neverland* will recall that a friendship, with them, inspired the creation of his now legendary work.

Actors can, though, wiggle them too much. *The Thick of It* and *In the Loop* star Peter Capaldi, missed out, evidently, on a place at The Royal Academy of Dramatic Art, because of his proclivity. Prior to finding stage and screen success, he auditioned there, in 1976, only to be told that his eyebrows were too active and his face too expressive. A curious decision, we might think, in a business that's all about expression, but he's admitted his tendency to, in those days, over-egg the pudding, describing himself as slightly larger than life, in his Shakespearean acting. In addition to numerous other achievements, he has since been awarded an Oscar; for his appearance in the short film, *Frank Kafka's It's a Wonderful Life.*

Windsor Davies, too, fell victim to his restless risers; well, almost. Once the highly vocal Sergeant Major 'Shut-up' Williams, looming large over his gang of 'lovely boys' and attendant 'Indians', in Croft and Perry's *It Ain't 'alf Hot Mum*; he found the transition, to straight acting, problematic. The difficulty arose during a death scene, when the facially quivering Sergeant Major threatened to put in an impromptu appearance. Davies had a problem, he has said, with his eye-brows. He'd become so used to twitching them that he struggled to keep them under control.

Sir Alec Guinness, on the other hand, may have had less difficulty. His *Our Man in Havana* performance was vividly described, by

Harland Kennedy, in *Film Comment* magazine. According to Kennedy, Guinness crouched; a vacuum cleaner salesman, deep in his own vacuum. Every five minutes an eyebrow would bob. Every ten, the voice would rouse itself to a new high, approximating to middle G.

We might think there are certain ways to address an octagenarian national treasure, but film maker John Landis is American and appeared to want none of it. *King Kong* and *Lord of the Rings* star, Andy Serkis described, to a *Time Out* journalist, his experience, on the set of Landis's *Burke* and *Hare* movie. The highlight, he recalled, had been watching John Landis directing Ronnie Corbett. The way John directs is, he explained, very forthright. His words to Corbett were, "Don't act with your fucking eyebrows Ronnie!"'

Fellow actor, David Hayman, incidentally, has spoken of his time spent working on that same film; referring, in particular, to his character's grisly death and the difficulty he experienced, in keeping a straight face. Ronnie Corbett walked in, Hayman said and did the funniest little cameos he'd seen, in cinema; yet, he had to lie, as if dead and not breathe, whilst trying to prevent himself from laughing.

The brow can, of course, conceal; to the frustration, sometimes, of observing journalists. Quentin Letts, of the Daily Mail noted that it was seldom easy to deduce much about the Trade Secretary, Vince Cable's moods, from the Commons gallery. He inspects the world, he wrote, from under two eyebrows, which perch on crags and conceal his inner mood. He wobbles his head and keeps his mouth pursed.

Tony Blair was another described well, when the former PM gave evidence, to the Leveson enquiry; a much publicised episode, which confirmed, astoundingly, that leading politicians had, indeed, hovered about the backside of Rupert Murdoch. Letts related many tics. His right eye-brow arched, like Norma Desmond. His horse like coughs, of sardonic disbelief. His piety, as he dropped his chin and stared ahead; eyeballs crossing.

Could this world ever be ready for such a close-up?

Furthermore, Blair's appearance was enlivened, by a courteous protestor, who apologised for interrupting proceedings, before branding his quarry a war criminal. Shocking, perhaps, for some, but a moment of level-browed satisfaction, probably, for many more.

When visiting a higher place, you might discover that cosmonaut and first man to orbit Earth, Yuri Gagarin, possessed a misshapen left eyebrow, but, sure as the stars, he didn't fall from space, to get it. The grand disfigurement occurred, instead, as he attempted to avoid his wife, Valentina. The incident followed a rowdy holiday, during which Gagarin decided to thrill some friends, with his motorboat antics. All well and good, you might think, but, during hostile weather, the great man's attempts to steer a straight course, left his hands damaged. Upon arrival, at a medical centre, he met Anna; an attractive, blonde nurse and later that same evening strayed from the marital bed, to visit her room. Desperate measures then saw our icon of the cosmos plunge to the ground, from a second floor balcony, permanently damaging his brow and probably not doing many favours for the vine, in which one of his feet became entangled. Not the most successful of missions then, but surely a spectacular one and upon rejoining the world of the ungiddy, he had only one question to ask: "will I fly again?"

What it is to fall for a nurse!

Should you venture into space, you may be unsurprised to find that planets do not have brows; except, that is, for Neptune; well, sort of. Following the discovery, in 1977, of rings, around its neighbour, Uranus, investigators identified, in 1984, a presence, close to Neptune. A complete ring-system, though, it was not. They were, instead, the arcing remnants of one; which have been likened to eyebrows, raised above the planet's surface. They remain observable, to this day.

But, that's science fact. What, you might ask, of science-fiction? If Mr Spock's eyebrows are not the most recognisable in screen history, they are surely the pointiest; yet producers, working for NBC, were uneasy, about revealing them, too soon. When first promoting *Star Trek*, they took the precaution of airbrushing them, from magazine photographs; together with his similarly eye-catching ears. The concern was that potential viewers would see Leonard Nimoy's character as satanic and so be dissuaded from giving the programme a chance. The strategy appears to have worked well; the

Star Trek programmes became some of the most successful in history and Mr Spock one of *NBC*'s most popular creations.

In Hollywood, Samuel Goldwyn was keen that Lana Turner should star in his movie *The Adventures of Marco Polo*. A golden opportunity, perhaps, but her involvement came at a high price; for Goldwyn demanded the removal of her eyebrows and replacement of them with fake, black ones. Sadly, they failed to re-grow and so she felt obliged to draw them, or paste on false ones, for the rest of her days. Lauren Bacall, however, managed to keep hers, but never knew why people considered her attractive; 'I always thought I had crooked eyebrows and crooked teeth' she said. That's why I never understood it when people called me a beauty'.

More recently, Jodie Marsh; the Essex glamour model and occasional butt of jokes, churned out by comedians, who've run out of other material, had her eyebrows permanently tattooed in 2008, for the benefit of *Children in Need*; proving she's more than the sum of her parts. Incidentally, since I've mentioned comedians, the late, great, Robin Williams suggested that Russian people love Brooke Shields, because her eyebrows remind them of Leonid Brezhnev.

James Newell Osterberg is better known to the world as Iggy Pop, a wild man of rock; but his chosen stage name has little to do with a style of music. It can be traced, instead, to his spell as a drummer, with a high-school band, known as the Iguanas; 'Iggy' being taken from their name. During his early days, with the Stooges, he would, then, be known as Iggy Stooge. Acquisition of the 'Pop' occurred later, when he shaved off his own eyebrows; comparisons having been drawn with a friend of the band, called Jimmy Pop; who'd lost all of his hair. Iggy's new look, however, had negative consequences. Upon performing with the Stooges, in their first paid gig, he not only painted his face, but applied an aluminium Afro arrangement, to his hair; a spectacle, I imagine, but during the course of the evening, his eyes were deluged with sweat, oil and fragmented metal, from his forehead; to the point of becoming severely swollen.

The precise method of the late, great, opera singer, Luciano Pavarotti, for increasing his upper-facial impact will be a mystery, to many; but John Allison, of *The Sunday Telegraph,* gained insight, when seeking to interview him, in Modena. He arrived to find staff applying lashings of black boot- polish to his eyebrows and hairline; all in anticipation of a photographer.

Alfred Hitchcock had intended not merely to film scenes for his *North by Northwest* movie upon Mount Rushmore, but to show a man dangling from one of Abraham Lincoln's eyebrows; but permission to shoot a chase sequence upon the great presidential faces was, alas, refused; so, a Hollywood set had to be used. And still with the movies, Bob Geldof is said to have experienced difficulty when filming the famous eyebrow-shaving moment in Pink Floyd's *The Wall*; and having performed the required act, felt an overwhelming compulsion to shave the rest of his body. That he did so was used, to great effect, within the film.

In this celebration of humanity's finest feature, I have understated, thus far, the attention that eyebrows can demand. Staff, at Portsmouth's Royal Naval Museum, will know where I'm coming from, because, having acquired their splendid wax-semblance of Lord Nelson, they were required to apply a touch of cosmetic surgery. Nelson, as many readers will know, lost an arm, in battle; together with sight, in his right eye; although he did not, in fact, wear an eye-patch; but sticklers for detail will wish me to point out that he also sustained significant brow damage. With much of the hair-producing tissue destroyed, he wore a half- brow, for the rest of his days. Additionally, it's believed that, in his later years, portrait artists thought to hide the imperfection, through favouring the other side of his face, or ensuring it remained concealed, by his other coverage.

The head lopping tyrant, still celebrated for his tenure as King Henry VIII, received a shock, to his right royal bonce, on the tenth day of March 1524, courtesy of a jousting accident. Upon that date, his majesty, whilst pratting around, with visor raised, was struck beneath his right brow, by the Duke of Suffolk. He continued to experience considerable pain, for the rest of his days; and it's been suggested that the incident turned him from relatively mild-mannered sovereign, to despot. The theory is a plausible one; and perish the thought that the United Kingdom's current monarch might have descended, in any way, from a frustrated butcher.

Four centuries on, in wartime Glamorgan, nobler brows were damaged; as can be learnt from Tom Clemett's account, in The Barry Gem newspaper. He described a build-up of troops and stockpiling, of weapons, around the Welsh town. Smoke screen canisters were many, which, when lit; at the onset of an air-raid; produced thick smoke; leaving houses covered with oily smudges. They sometimes caught fire and the air raid warden extinguished the flames. He was, said Clemett, easily identifiable, by his singed eyebrows and other hair.

The United Kingdom contains many anatomical place-names. We could visit Liphook, in Sussex; Pratt's Bottom, or how about Kneesworth? As for Prickwillow; well, with apologies to its residents, let's not go there (nor Pratt's Bottom, for that matter). Anyway, we're searching for finer things, so how about a trip across the pond, to the obscure Kentucky town, known as Monkey's Eyebrow? The origin of its name has yet to be established, but may have something to do with Ballard County resembling, in shape, the head of a primate. The town in question can be seen, on maps, as the animal's eyebrow (imagining, of course, that monkeys possess such things). It is known, however, that there were once two Monkey's Eyebrows; referred to as Old Monkey and New Monkey; and that's pretty much it.

But why not dispense with the monkey-business anyway and cross the nation's border, to the Canadian province of Saskatchewan? There, at the intersection of highways 42 and 367, we would find the village simply named 'Eyebrow'; and this time, a real, geographical, feature; a hill, of said shape, looming over a lake, also finely named. You may, perhaps, wish to holiday there. I do.

Those who dream of eyebrows; and readers may be surprised to learn that I don't; may wish to understand the meanings of their visions. Dream interpretation is, of course, an inexact science and opinion varies, greatly. Perusing the internet, I unearthed a suggestion that dreams containing eyebrows mean we are 'worried, or dissatisfied with either someone, or something' (nothing earth-shattering there, because who isn't?). A gender identity crisis is more specific and if you're a forty-something male, who, having experienced such a dream, awakens in his wife's shoes, it can reasonably be seen as evidence. Dreams of people without eyebrows are said to indicate the loss of sexual function, while visions of them partially shaven suggest low self-esteem, lack of confidence and, more worryingly, castration anxiety; a fair reason, surely, to board up your door and note the postman's tendency to look at you in a funny way. Imagining, in dreams, that you possess a unibrow denotes, it's said, insecurity regarding your physical appearance, or, alternatively, that you are not properly expressing your emotions. It is all, of course, highly speculative and claims that we will encounter obstacles, in the near future, either state the obvious, or are mere superstition; which is where I tend to draw the line.

Recognition of the forehead, as a salt dispenser, can be traced, back, through many years; all the way, in fact, to the Bible. In Genesis, Adam is caught with some semblance of cider around his gills; causing 'the Almighty'; ever the charmer; to throw the mother of all tantrums: *"Cursed is the ground because of you; through painful toil you will eat food from it, all the days of your life. It will produce thorns and thistles for you and you will eat the plants of the field. By the sweat of your brow, you will eat your food until you return to the ground, since from it you were taken; for dust you are and to dust you will return."*

Considering his proclaimed pre-eminence as creator of the universe, we might wonder who rattled his cage.

John McEnroe, on the other hand, was more subdued, in his outbursts, on Centre Court. His own frons was unremarkable; unlike that of Boris Becker. Benji Wilson, of *The Telegraph,* extolled the German's finest features, in 2009 and predicted momentous events. Becker's eyebrows were, he said, a magnificent sight in full-flow. He speculated, too, that they may, upon closure of a new roof, rise so high as to join his hairline and form a magnificent new landmass

Ancient China's *Red Eyebrow Rebellion* did not, somewhat disappointingly, involve a bunch of miscreant and painted teenagers, breaking into the school tuck-shop; rather, a sector of the population attempting to free themselves, from poverty. A spectacular crew; with not merely their brows reddened, but much of the forehead too, they defeated the army of Wang Mang and in so doing, played their part in reinstating the Han dynasty. Disarray would, however, follow, as civil war ensued; the 'Red Eyebrows' then attempting to install a descendent of the Liu clan. But, with their tendency to appoint the illiterate and raid towns, with little regard for any infrastructure, they are best described as inept. Finally, they would fall; defeated by the army of emperor Guangwu; leaving a legacy of disruption, mismanagement and unforgiveable garishness.

Whilst applying the slap-on is considered, by some modern puritans, distasteful, even they would hardly called it a crime. Not so, in ancient China, where metropolitan governor Zhang Chang, became the first person to be charged with elicit cosmetology; a bizarre apprehension, we might think; and still more so, because the enhancement was applied, not to his own features, but those of his spouse. Such censure came courteous of the Western Han Dynasty, whose rulers got all hot and sour, upon discovering that one of its servants had, each day, enhanced his wife's eyebrows. Publicly disgraced, the overly artistic Zhang found himself whisked away and in an episode sufficient to send a prawn crackers, or make a spring roll, was hauled before Emperor Xuandi. There, he found himself on something of a sticky wicket. In performing an act of beautification, upon a woman, he had transgressed a formal rule of conduct; yet his maligned ribs were to be spared, because Zhang quite simply chose to remind the Emperor of the proverbial birds and bees; thus lessening the gravity of his offence. A short while later, the sour turned to sweet, when, having further argued that his affairs were his own, Zhang found that freedom was securely in the bag. Never again was he promoted, but many commoners found his story touching. Chang Zhang's tracing of his wife's eyebrows became a popular tale of marital love; to be retold, even in the form of an opera; presumably one void of bargain-basement humour.

Issues of the brow are rare, in British sport; save for the occasional cricketer retiring hurt, in those days before they donned helmets and made us guess who they are; yet, in Japan, certain sensibilities clearly exist, as we can tell from a story, which appeared, in that nation's version of *The Times.* Six junior high school students were, it seems, disqualified from a Tochigi prefectural judo tournament, on the grounds that their thin eyebrows went against rules.

According to the Prefectural Sports Federation for Junior High Schools, which organized the event, officials saw more than ten students with thin eyebrows, as they carried out pre-match checks of students' weight and judo suits.

After questioning the students, match officials decided to disqualify six students, who were determined to have deliberately thinned out their eyebrows, by plucking them or shaving them, the federation said. Tatsuo Kakizaki, head of the federation's judo department, defended the action, saying that thin eyebrows are banned "because they intimidate and are unpleasant for the opponent."

Anything goes, in most western nations, including, in boxing, the frequent coating of eyebrows with petroleum-jelly (*Vaseline*). This is not, however, a sign of vanity run riot; rather an attempt to reduce friction and so help prevent the skin from splitting. Quite simply, the opponents glove slides away, sparing his adversary the flow of blood that might otherwise fog his vision and cost him victory.

Less sportingly, that Ron Paul's alleged eyebrow malfunction caused a furore should surprise no one. It is, of course, not the done thing to expose a falsie; particularly if you're aiming to become US president. Even so, amid the inconsistencies, gaffs and Sarah Palin-style calamities that peppered the way to Trump, it should hardly rank as a slip; yet *YouTube* clips abounded; with attention to detail best reserved for weapons of mass destruction. The truth of it was unclear. Maybe Paul did wear them; or is it just that Republican candidates are naturally thicker?

Without wishing to draw an obvious connection, the late American comedian Bill Hicks had a novel take on issues of the brow:

"You ever noticed how people who believe in Creationism look really unevolved? You ever noticed that? Eyes real close together, eyebrow ridges, big furry hands and feet. 'I believe God created me in one day'. Yeah, looks like he rushed it."

Eyebrows are, of course, the business of comedians. Their careers hinge upon getting them to shift, one way or another. The unmoved forehead confronts them, surely, as the enemy; an unconditional sign of failure; and many traditional stand-ups aim for an instantaneous laugh; where the brow's concerned, something quite close to furrowing. With others, the game is more akin to felling cricket-stumps. Arches rise, before they fall; never to be disturbed, again, by the same degree of distasteful content; so he, or she, ploughs on;

mining yet greater depths. Are we seeing, then, a laudable pioneer, pushing the boundaries of what's arguably an art-form, or does the toppling begin to grate? Sure as heck, jokes about people hurling themselves before trains would be unwelcome in the homes of grieving relatives; whether anticipated or not, but does that render them polluters? I'll merely observe that some humorists have raised the roof, without lifting a single brow.

It may be bonkers to suggest that New York's Statue of Liberty wears the brows of Lucifer; yet, those who proffer it, make at least one valid point, because, facially, the figure does look very male. The forehead, in particular, is furrowed, notably angular and connects with a lengthy nose. The brows, themselves, are strikingly low; something else we would expect to see upon the male form; and of course, the figure does bear a torch fit for Lucifer. Allegations of occult symbolism, in France's generous gift to the USA, are for a different book. Even so, the more I look; the more convinced I become that they are, indeed, the brows of a man.

"Christ!...he's been struck by lightning!" Words taken, perhaps, from a cricketing, or golfing anecdote? Actually, no; although they may have featured in one. For this tale is on a grander scale. Created many years before Nectar points, and even Green Shield Stamps, few would deny that *Christ the Redeemer*; overlooking the sun-kissed city of Rio de Janeiro; is an impressive sight. It is, though, extraordinarily elevated and exposed and hardly surprising that such a tourist-attraction would be struck, by lightning, in a less than mysterious way. Much would be made, in the year 2008, of the redeemer's ability to remain unscathed. Miracles are, after all, difficult to find. Anyway, the big guy's eyebrows were damaged; together with his fingers; leaving him in need of significant restoration.

A final issue of the brow and this time a linguistic one. It has been said that a staggering twenty-seven words are used in Albania to describe the eyebrow; although I must confess to not having caught a plane, to check. Some things are a touch beyond the call of duty.

They do, though, include *vetullosh* (very thick eyebrows); *vetullan* (very bushy ones); *vetullor* (those that are slightly arched)

Other languages, of course, contain their own relevant nouns; albeit more straightforward ones; and in case you feel inclined to tear around the globe, like Michael Palin's over-caffeined twin, whilst chin-wagging about the brow, here are some of them:

Albanian – Vetull (pronounced *vetool)*

Catalan – Cella (readers of a certain age may wish to think of the frizzy haired singer Leo Sa*yer*...well, perhaps)

Croatian - Obrva (as it's spelt, with every letter clearly pronounced, making a rattling sound)

Dutch -   Wenkbrauw (the *'w'* sounding more like an *'l'* and the *'e'* like an *'i'*...so *linkbrow)*

Finnish - Kulmakarva (every letter pronounced, but an *'ooh'* sound from the *'u'*)

French – Sourcil (source*eel)*

German - Augenbrau (*augenbrower*)

Indonesian – Alis *(allee)*

Italian – Sopracciglio (sopra*cheeyo)*

Latvian – Uzacs *(oozas)*

Maltese – Eyebrow (for those who insist on playing it safe)

Polish – Brew (more like *breath)*

Portuguese – Sobrancelha (sobran*selyea)*

Spanish – Ceja *(sayha)*

Welsh – Ael (like *isle)*

Chapter 6   Beautifying the Brow

You may already have seen mention, within these pages, of brow-beautification's long history; yet it can be traced back further than one might imagine. Indeed, ancient art suggests that people, in Mesopotamia removed unwanted hair, from their brows; while an excavation, of Ur, in ancient Sumer, has revealed rudimentary tweezers, within a tomb believed to have been constructed way back, in 3500BC. Certainly, it's thought that many women in ancient Greece (circa 3000 BC) wore fake-eyebrows, made from oxen hair; and by 1500 BC, Romans were blackening theirs, with antimony and soot. They preferred dark eyebrows, that almost met in the center and the effect was achieved, by darkening and then extending them, inwards. Plucking began, in the first century BC, to tidy the overall look.

The practice of eyebrow removal and their replacement, with applied substances, is also long-established; particularly in Japan, where it has been ascribed a name. The word *Hikimayu* was formed by combining two others: *hiki*, meaning 'pull' and *mayu*, which means 'eyebrows' Popular among aristocracy, the process involved application of *haizumi*; a powdered ink, made from soot; taken from sesame seed oil. The Chinese, however, got there first. It was one of several trends adopted, from them, by the Japanese; including whitening of the face, with *oshiroi* powder. Initially, high arcs would be painted, but, during the Heian period, experimentation led to the wearing of smudged oval shapes and by the twelfth century, men, too, had caught the fashion bug; creating similar looks, for themselves. Hikimayu, by this point, was well established and although male engagement would lessen, it remained popular, among women, for many centuries. The Edo period, in the seventeenth century, brought a change, though, with hikimayu only considered permissible for those who were married and by the mid to late nineteenth century western cultural influences dominated; in 1870 it would be banned, from society, to re-emerge only occasionally, at festivals and in historical drama.

If we were to also visit China, it may surprise us to hear mention of an ancient proverb: *'The silkworm-moth eyebrow of a woman is the axe that cuts down the wisdom of man.'* A curious one, you might think, but it's easily explained; for the silkworm carries ornate, feather- like, antennae; which bear a gilded appearance. Seen head on, they look rather like beautiful eyebrows: so, in order to understand the proverb, we need to think in terms of a beguiling femme fatale; not the way we generally view the soberly coloured insects that cling to our curtains.

Back in the UK and perhaps a few other countries, a new trend has emerged. Tattooed eyebrows clearly save time; and with the likes of Dame Helen Mirren acquiring them, could be seen, more and more. The tattoos concern individual hair strokes, drawn in semi-permanent ink, to give realistic-looking eyebrows, without the need to apply a pencil, powder, or gel. Dame Helen had become, she has said, fed up of her brows being barely there and thought the replacements looked great on a friend. The Oscar winning actress paid fresh attention to hers, upon playing the Queen, in Peter

Morgan's *The Audience*. She has quite present eyebrows, Mirren observed and when making herself up, found the look interesting.

The younger royals have generated interest too. The Duchess of Cambridge's eyebrows are widely admired; particularly since she transformed them. Kate's brow guru, Sabrina Eleonore has spoken, to *Hello!* Magazine, of the process. Kate, she told a journalist, has naturally dark and fairly thick brows, but wears them in a way that's neat, but natural looking.

Sabrina uses various methods, to achieve the look, including microblading, waxing and pencilling.

And the Duchess of Sussex is said to have debuted a new eyebrow-style, at Royal Ascot, although it might not quite be so. She over-tweezed them, it's been suggested, before allowing them to grow back. Megan, has, like Kate, a brow-stylist, who may tint them; yet, some observers suspect the use of brow powder; and that her make-up artist applied, for the royal wedding, a new shade.

In Elizabethan England, women had higher concerns than their eyebrows. Fashion being a curious entity; high foreheads were much sought after and hairlines would often be plucked, to acquire them. Walnut oil was sometimes even applied to the foreheads of children, in order to pre-empt a perceived problem, through stemming growth and less frequently, bandages coated with vinegar and cat dung, too.

A shift in emphasis made Georgian women more attentive to their brows, although, rather than plucking and darkening, they would thicken and lighten them. Still more surprisingly, the favoured colour was grey; so securing mouse hair, with adhesive, made perfect sense; to the female mind, anyway. Thickening can also be achieved, it is said, by applying castor oil, prior to sleep. The process is believed to be particularly useful in stimulating re-growth, where brows have been over-plucked, and can also have a darkening effect.

Those who do wish to pluck, but have sensitive skin, may favour eyebrow-threading. Although popular in the middle-east and parts of

Asia, for centuries, its presence, within western nations, has emerged only recently. Even so, endorsement of the process, by celebrities such as Reese Witherspoon and Selma Hayek, suggests that we'll be seeing a lot more of it. Regarded, by many, as an art form, threading involves the dexterous twisting of cotton, within the eyebrow. In so doing, the practitioner is able to trap and gently remove each hair, achieving greater precision than with other methods. The arched eyebrow, in particular, can, then, be better created.

And those who can't be bothered with the fuss of it may wish to embrace the perhaps somewhat harsh words of American preacher and civil rights activist, Jesse Jackson: "Life is too short to spend hoping that the perfectly arched eyebrow or hottest new lip shade will mask an ugly heart."

A Few Memorable Brow Raisers

1977 - While being grilled, by David Frost, Richard Nixon insists that when the President does it, it's not illegal; thus publicly declaring his presumed right, while in office, to transgress democratic law.

Two years later, newly elected prime-minister, Margaret Thatcher, stands in Downing Street and quotes St Francis of Assisi: "Where there is discord may we bring harmony…" Her years of power were some of the most divisive in modern times; bringing pitch battles over pit closures, the poll-tax riots and unemployment raised to more than three million.

Rumours circulate, during the 1980s, that much-loved *Blockbusters* presenter, Bob Holness, had been the saxophone player, on Gerry Rafferty's classic, *Baker Street*; causing music lovers to all but have a P in their astonishment. Sadly, it was an urban myth.

1981 - Labour leader, Michael Foot, wears something akin to a donkey jacket, beside the Cenotaph; sending Fleet Street editors into salivation overload. The coat had been bought by Foot's wife and was thought smart by the Queen Mother. Even so, he could have chosen better.

Also in 1981, the Prince of Wales announces his engagement to Lady Diana Spencer and utters the ominous words "whatever in love means". Did alarm bells ring? If so, they were well hidden.

1997 - World leaders pay their sorry tributes, to deceased Chinese president Deng Xiaoping; responsible, surely, for the Tiananmen Square massacre. Among them is British Prime Minister, John Major. He informs audiences that Deng "played a key role, in the process, which led to the Joint Declaration on Hong Kong, in 1984, embodying his visionary concept of one country, two systems." A few well-chosen expletives might, for once, have been excusable and far more appropriate.

1998 - Errant US President, William Jefferson Clinton tests the English language, by declaring that he "… did not have sexual relations with that woman, Miss Lewinsky". He subsequently owns up; having accepted that a cake's still a cake, even when the marzipan stays on the plate.

Martin Creed wins the 2001 Turner Prize, with his work entitled *The Lights Going on and Off,* which is, in fact, an empty room, with... you've guessed it... the lights going on and off. Art so rarely does exactly what it 'says on the tin'.

2009 - Bushy eyebrowed and somewhat dowdy spinster strolls onto the set of a UK talent show, launches into that song from *Les Miserables* and fifteen seconds later, Britain's got coffee stains on the carpet. Whatever our take on Susan Boyle, she provided a memorable moment in the history of reality television.

2007 - Despite being responsible for countless civilian deaths, in Iraq, Tony Blair is made a middle-east peace-envoy.

1986 - Events within an entire series of *Dallas* (that's 31 episodes) are nullified, when viewers are told it's all been a dream. Having woken, Pam Ewing re-encounters her murdered husband, Bobby, in the shower. You couldn't, or, at least, wouldn't, make it up.

2008 - While being interviewed, for *GQ* magazine, Liberal Democrat leader Nick Clegg speaks of his thirty sexual conquests; as the ghost of Marvin Gaye plays a private gig inside his head.

1979 - During a televised discussion, concerning Monty Python's *The Life of Brian*, evangelical journalist, Malcolm Muggeridge, declares "there's nothing in this film that could destroy anyone's faith, because it's much too tenth rate for that." In today's more secular society, it remains one of the best loved movies.

2010 - At a papal reception, The Duke of Edinburgh asks Scottish Conservative leader Annabel Goldie if she's wearing tartan knickers; proving that, despite his gaffs and apparent irascibility, he does, actually, possess an admirable sense of humour.

Some Brow Furrowers

1982 - Henry VIII's flagship *The Mary Rose* is raised, from the Solent. Those of us with runaway imaginations are disappointed, when it turns out not to have shiny cannons and unfurling sails. In reality, it's closer to a pile of driftwood.

At Twickenham, also in 1982, Erica Roe adds excitement to rugby, through revealing wonders much more inspiring than a full back; but England's unofficial mascot Ken Bailey covers her commendable props with a Union Flag.

1984 - The sunshine ends, in May, as Eric Morecambe's death is announced. Television producers ease our furrowed brows by screening, repeatedly, Eric and Ernie's grapefruit-cleaving, sausage-twirling, kitchen routine.

In 1990, *Marathon* bars are nonsensically renamed *Snickers*; dashing all hopes that they might, one day, reach 26 miles, 385 yards in length.

1993 - A calamitous cock-up, at the Aintree starting-line, sees a large field tear twice around the track; leaping, majestically, over Becher's Brook and the Chair, before jockey John White, caked in mud, arrives, triumphant. A minute or so later, he learns that he and those who backed his mount have won nothing at all. The race was declared void.

1999 - Hordes of adventurers journey to Devon and Cornwall, for a brief burst of the dawn chorus; a pleasant enough experience, we might think, but it was eleven in the morning and they were there to witness a total eclipse of the sun. Proving themselves true Brits, they cheered anyway; despite the heavy cloud-cover.

Wimbledon 1990 and Sir Cliff Richard enacts his plot to entertain rain-sodden tennis fans, gathered on Centre Court. Some, no doubt, are thrilled, while others pray for a peaceful exit.

2005 - Prime Minister to be, David Cameron, declares his support for the bombing of Iraq; although with a *heavy heart*. The weight of his less than pertinent blood pump may be of interest to somebody.

Members of Britain's twitching community descend upon the town of Grimsby, in 2004, to glimpse an American Robin, only to see it snatched away by a Sparrowhawk. Northern hospitality is rarely so harsh.

7/7/2005 - As the Iraq war continues, four young men; their heads filled with certainty and their back-packs explosives, journey, to London, on their deadly mission. Our furrowed brows are not enough and prayers are said, in churches throughout the land. Meanwhile, many long for a true age of reason.

Songs of the Brow

Diana Ross and The Supremes - Ain't No Mountain High Enough (...to top your

eyebrows)

Jackie Wilson - Higher and Higher (for all who aspire to greatness)

Elvis Presley - Way Down (for those more into 'gurning')

George Michael - Careless Whisper (for those with chocolate in their

brows)

B J Thomas - Raindrops Keep Falling On My Head (but that doesn't mean the amount   of water meeting with my eyes won't be very slightly reduced, due to my evolved eyebrows)

Rod Stewart - The First Cut is the Deepest (so leave them alone and shave your chin

instead)

James Taylor – Will you still love me tomorrow? (when I've shaved off my eyebrows)

Spice Girls - Two Become One (for ageing wearers of the monobrow)

Ronan Keating - When you Say Nothing at All (your eyebrows tend to twitch)

The Beatles – All My Loving (I will send to you; together with a small quantity of eyebrow clippings)

The Rolling Stones - Paint it Black (for the mildly experimental)

The Police - Don't Stand So Close To Me (because my eyebrows told you not to)

Randy Newman –You Can Leave Your Hat On (because it hides your unusually ugly eyebrows)

Roberta Flack - The First Time Ever I Saw Your Face (I really dug your eyebrows)

The Fabulous Furry Eyebrows - You Raise Me up (well, maybe)

Anything by *The Levellers*, or *Joe Cocker*.

Superfluous eyebrow frolics

Doctor, doctor, I've just been stung on the eyebrow!

Well, have you considered shopping somewhere less surreal, instead?

My girlfriend says nobody can top my eyebrows!

Is it just a haircut, or do you want 'hundreds and thousands' as well?

Doctor, doctor, my eyebrows are always soaking wet!

Take this to the chemist... and any chance of cleaning the windows on your way out?

Mummy, why are you always plucking your eyebrows?

Because Daddy keeps nicking my banjo, dear!

Doctor, doctor, I keep finding twenty pound notes in my eyebrows!

No change there then!

Doctor, doctor, I can't wiggle my eyebrows!

Well, why have you come to me? There's a book about that sort of thing. I recommend a few pages, each day (well, I would, wouldn't I?), together with lots of practice and if that doesn't do the trick, you'll have my unwavering sympathy.

Thanks for having a browse ;-)

Printed in Great Britain
by Amazon